I0756246

FINISHING LINE PRESS
www.finishinglinepress.com

Sonnets For Agnodice

poems by

Mark Novak

Finishing Line Press
Georgetown, Kentucky

Sonnets For Agnodice

ISBN 979-8-89990-483-7 First Edition

ACKNOWLEDGMENTS

'Robin Williams' first appeared in the *Bards*, San Francisco Anthology
'$50' first appeared in the *Miserere Review*
'Fucked Up' and 'Surquedry,'first appeared in the Cocktales Literary pages of *DearBooze.com*
'I Stole a Bottle of Whiskey from the Cartel' first appeared in the pages of the *Underland Review*

Publisher: Leah Huete de Maines
Editor: Christen Kincaid
Cover Art: Chloe Liao
Author Photo: Ray Raisedana
Cover Design: Elizabeth Maines McCleavy

Order online: www.finishinglinepress.com
also available on amazon.com

Author inquiries and mail orders:
Finishing Line Press
PO Box 1626
Georgetown, Kentucky 40324
USA

Contents

Sonnets for Agnodice

1.

Agnodice's folded fist lifts her tunic
Lo, there, the pubis of her sisterhood!
Lie back lady, let her tend to the sick,
The menses and migraines of the matured.
Tend to birth-dreams of a new world order.
Invisible-citizen—practitioner.
Courageous, Sappho pens praises for her,
As Herophilus quakes for what unfolds here.
Strap your breasts and cut the locks, clip thy sex!
'Tis the business of Gods and men to heal.
In guise of male you work and project,
Passion to cure a city-state concealed.
The head is crowning like a gold sunrise,
While convened Senate wipe sleep from their eyes.

2.

Agnodice's folded fist lifts her tunic
Lo! Orbs of men, there is no member there.
For shame, physicians squall, to treat and mix
In medicine, for all here to compare.
The audacity! *Bring Herophilus*
Forward! Frankenstein crafts his vile she-male.
Women of Athens, I have no phallus,
Yet, answer me: Have I Not Healed You Well!?
Wilt thou three times deny thy creation!?
Buckle beneath the jealousies of these men?
Deny my drams, plants and operations!?
Is this Golden Age without transcendence?
"Hold Thy Tongues!" Cries the voice of Aspasia.
Before these judgments, a defense of the ages.

3.

Agnodice's folded fist drops her tunic.
"Know now the talent of this physician,"
The powerhouse roars with eyes volcanic,
"Hear these accounts before rendered decisions…
Know you my son, and the wrath of his father!?
By these skilled hands the younger was delivered!!
Would you destroy gifts given by nature?
For Shame! I say, a wolf is your shepherd.
Young Pericles was stuck, not to be moved,
Blood cord about the neck when he was born,
'Twas these hands that turned the babe and renewed
Nature's course, and your prince was thereby spawned.
Think before you issue these poisoned herbs!
Your judgments by the king's ear shall be heard."

4.

Agnodice's hem sweeps earth—broom turned tunic.
Seated here before the law of Athens,
Throngs of women, those cured—witness'd public.
Agonized cough and shift, the Senate spasms.
Bloodied bird in hand, now catch and release,
How to inoculate Aspasia's rage?
To win back favor of the king and priests.
Societal bends as steel in a swage.
Retire then council, measures and weights,
Banish the damned, or let be acquitted?
Choke on male pride, this accusative case,
Agnodice's skills are hereby permitted—
So, nurse the Polis, it's sick and diseased,
Neutralized sex, by decree o' Pericles.

$50.

We were howling in the urine stained
Streets of the Tenderloin
He was an old, black man. Homeless.
Short cropped, white hair and beard;
Sitting in his wheelchair with piercing eyes
And those thick wrinkles forged in Vietnam…
We sounded good together.
He took the high part,
I harmonized the low end.
My Girl.
The Temptations.

We sustained the final interval,
Blooming the breaths
of those two final notes,
And then we laughed…
Congratulated ourselves.
Shook hands and called each other, Brother.

Before departing ways, he said,
"You Got $50 I Can Have!?"
I laughed and said, "No, Man,
I Ain't Got $50 To Give You!"
He sighed deeply and consigned,
"Alright, ...I'll take $20 then."

Psalm of Billy Hofer

(Extinction of the Last Herd)

Eleven of the last bison dead,
Five skinned in the crimson snow.
Six heads dangle in the lodgepoles,
Extinction of the last herd
in Yellowstone.

In the year that Taylor was inaugurated,
and the Minnesota Territory was drawn,
Your first dawn rose from the Atlantic horizon
and fell above a newly ratified California.

In hindsight, casting the long stretch of national shadow,
squinting hard into the distance of time, we plainly see,
the place where your life develops its manifest destiny.

Hoist and sail from civilizing demands of New England.
Charting further to challenges of some rougher existence.

Give me the West!
The Bear and the Wolf!!
—Follow The Star Course…
—Go West, Young Man!
Take your callused hands,
Take your voracious appetites
For books and hard adventure,
—And Go West!

How Marvelous! What A Time To Be Alive!
How A Man May Reach The Frontier In Days!
A new landscape requires the grit and strength of your youth,
testing that wiry physique as you strap on Norwegian shoes
and carry those parcels of your newly invested purpose:

"Neither snow nor rain nor heat nor gloom of night
stays these couriers from the swift completion of their appointed rounds."

From Tellurium, Colorado to Animas Forks, you make the Grizzly Pass.
Making your peace with the territorial entrenchment of mountain goats.
Gloved-frostbite, howling winds—forces of blizzard and avalanche.
Yet, ask yourself—is this enough!?

Your adventurous heart
Uncontainably yearns…

Did you travel this distance only to sponge predictability and routine!?
To blend in Denver's rising assemblage, now some 5,000 residents?
A government messenger on skis,
Serving this newly growing populace.

Eleven of the last bison dead,
Five skinned in the crimson snow.
Six heads dangle in the lodgepoles,
Extinction of the last herd
in Yellowstone.

Your days in the Black Hills prove no more fruitful,
The greatest stakes are always the first lots claimed…
Levi and the Giant Four knew better.
Fuel the hungers of the wanting seeds…
That's where the real gold hides.

In Scribner's Magazine, you learn of this wondrous new wild,
Grant sets aside two million acres, and your bones are aching—

To see the treasure, the land,
the people, the collection of animals.
Game and opportunity…

And anyway—you sigh—scratch at your dark mustache,
—the best stakes are gone…
And the train is boarding for Bozeman.

In Montana fortune smiles, the sun crests over Rocky peaks,
you find yourself dining in the company of ambitious Col. Pickett.

Laws of Chemistry:
  Like minds attract.
The sportsman knows the desolate wild you seek,
  and requires a pack-hand.
You dive deep in your element,
in your sober hunger to commune,

To hunt and gather and survive
the uninhabitable.

And while Pickett returns to his ranch,
with trophies and hides,
To his political ambition and connections—you stay
on to find yourself,
To grow like a thermophile
bubbling in a hot spring.

Norris gifts to you, revelations.
Setting the hook.
Book-primed as a geyser jet.
All things of beauty
are derived from pressure.

From Gardiner your tenure begins:
How then, to keep this land wild??
Preserve what should always be frontier?

Rail Tycoons and Thunderclap.
Corporate famines of the East.
A Ravenous Crush of Money Graze.
All things indigenous must be cleared.
Bringing death: to Indians, Elk and Buffalo.
Elders lament of numerical majesty
That the Great Plains once did boast,
Before the Great Genocide unloaded.

Specters hold court in your head…
Where are they now? Those legendary bison herds,
Reduction and scarcity—Death Rattle.
Extinction in Yellowstone?

Grinnel, editor of Forest and Stream,
Sends you an Anthony Camera,
Enclosure letter of congratulations:
You are the newest part of the team!
Perhaps the sharpest tool in his box!?
"Our Man On The Ground…"

All the conservationists of the East
Depend upon your scribblings.
Your romanticized reports and
Descriptives of nature's cathedrals,
Words pack the power.
Words: might emblazon the interests
Nurture protections of this wild land.
Crown jewel of ecological marvel.

The Northern-Pacific rails forth the wealthy,
and you line your pockets for the winter stores.
Platformed as the premiere set of boots and eyes.
To guide the privileged before this inhospitable,
and hard natural wonder.

Eleven of the last bison dead,
Five skinned in the crimson snow.
Six heads dangle in the lodgepoles,
Extinction of the last herd
in Yellowstone.

Grinnel sends you a young associate.
President of Club Boone and Crocket.
A conservation society, nascent-ariel,
Helmed by young upstart, Theodore Roosevelt.
The man is intent to see this No-Man's Land:
Fin, Wing, and Beast. And the Nirvana, you give him
sets his passions ablaze!

Juices of mad ambition pump through his monstrous brain
As he straddles the Continental Divide, watching
Two Oceans run between his feet,
Feeding the Snake and Mississippi...
Both Atlantic and Pacific, feel the tug of his line...

He returns to New York, In the glow of purpose...
—determined to birth and nourish protections
to this sacred ground.
Your wish in his vision.

A walking tour is proposed,
Get word to the world! Printing
to the nation's 38 million residents!
Increase the intrigue,
the visitations,
Then the protections.
—Are sure to follow...

...As will the huntsman.
—As will the poachers.

A census is to be taken of the wildlife
numbers. Estimate the elk, the moose,
find some bison. ...if you can?

The military is stationed to patrol
this massive acreage, and you are
commissioned to teach the skills of
Norwegian skiing to these troops,

On completion you set off for blizzards.
Winds and powders.
Toting your pencils and pads,
and the weighted load
of a Plate Anthony Camera.
Seeking the last members
of the last herd of Yellowstone.

A transient sportsman skirts the road,
Past the checkpoints
of a security theater,
The scarcity of the stock
has increased the values.
Smith's supply and demand.

$1,000 for the head of a bison will keep him in comfort,
And so, Edward Howell, toils through razor bite of snow,
Dragging his frozen sled of supplies, ammunition and rifles,

To his delight,
After days of frozen toil,

Effort finds reward.
Preparation & Opportunity.
He finds them there,
—past the Canyon and Falls.

Silent and grazing, in slow majestic chew.
Large and as ominous as buckboards,
those massive humps of high-pile shag,
soil earth tones of loam cascading down
in thick winter coats to darker hues
that hang from their mandibles,
Hair fibers from shoulders to hooves.
Biting. Pulling at sparse frozen vegetation.
Intent on hard forage and survival.

Rib cages arise and expand, those big lungs,
cold mists blooming out in snorts of existence.
Beneath regal horns that point upward: Heavenly—
those dark, wide eyes of innocence focus
across the impossible wind-blown drifts,
as Edward Howell unshoulders his rifle,
sights the beasts upon his barrel, and opens fire…

The shots ring and echo in the ice-crisp air,
Capturing the attention of the nearby patrol squad.
fulfilling their orders to keep hunters away,
They trudge in his direction until at ghastly last,
they find him there, with blood on his hands,
and the grisly mess of massacre before his feet.

Eleven of the last bison dead,
Five skinned in the crimson snow.
Six heads dangle in the lodgepoles,
Extinction of the last herd
in Yellowstone.

Shocked. Howel awakens from skinning concentrations,
To the barrel of the squad—so little so late—pointed at his temple.
As he suffers in the frigidity of the military holding cell in Mammoth,
biding his time and awaiting the release for his minor misdemeanor,

Roosevelt and Vest have set the wheels of Washington in motion.
A bully-hard avengement to the dark void of Howell's atrocities,
Crimes and murder, Rep. Lacey
Presents his bill to Congress,
And Cleveland signs it into law.
At last, the hunted bare their teeth.

In aftermath,
the Smithsonian calls
for protection numbers…
Your scarce Wonderland census.
Estimate: 200 bison heads remain.
To repopulate this dying herd.
You make to build a palisade,
A paddock of desperate action
An impossible solution…

Bison go where they choose.

The domain of Yellowstone
with Laws of Man must conjoin…

Ark of the covenant
To protect and steward
the animals,
and pray that they breed.
Breed and roam.

Roam as a young Hofer once did…
Now an "Uncle" to the Park.
You ponder in the autumn cold,
How long can any animal exist
In these dramatic hardships?
Do the Nez Perce,
have need of tribe?

Increase in interest…
in population….
in profit—

has nourished
young protections.

  You deserve your rest.
    Do you not?

Reflections of your Manifest Destiny.
You have not yet made the Pacific…

Eye your baited line,
Your minor retirement.
Follow the salmon.

You have skills
to service,
community.
in a humble life,
with nature anew:

 The Eagle.
  The Orca
—No longer a pack
  leader perhaps?
—Expectations change.
—Terminus shifts.
—And look at this view
from Whidbey Isle!

While dreaming on the Great Herds,
and those few members that still remain…

Eleven of the last bison dead,
Five skinned in the crimson snow.
Six heads dangle in the lodgepoles,
Extinction of the last herd
in Yellowstone.

**(Inspired by the book: Yellowstone's Lost Legend. Much thanks to Prof. Scott Herring, UC Davis, for directing me in additional points of research.)*

The Gold-Toothed Woman

In Curacao:
The biggest woman
I've ever met.
6 feet, 5 inches
She made me
feel petite.

She had dark,
silk skin.
Like velvet.
Like chocolate.

She wore a saya
And a headwrap.
High manicured brows
With a gold-tooth smile.
She was a woman
who knew what
she wanted.

And she was going
to get it, too....

"Well now," she charmed,
"How is it you are here
With no woman
To gobble you up!?
I might take you
home for myself..."

I was moved to smile,
she flashed back her gold,
Brilliance behind
big, beautiful lips.

"If you already
have a woman,"
She elaborated,
"I'll share you with her,
I'm not selfish, Love.
I don't get jealous."

She put out her hand
For me,
Probing her offering.
A woman. Who knows…

I put my credit card
In her palm,
And she moved me
To the cash register.

She was a
gold-tooth woman,
Who knew
What she wanted.

And she was going
to get it, too…

I Stole a Bottle of Whiskey From The Cartel

I stole a bottle of whiskey from the cartel. I was drunk—and high. But I'm still here to tell the tale as no dead man could. Trump said they're eating pets in Springfield, like locusts, en como un viruses, it made my girl ill, or perhaps it was Montezuma's revenge?? No diferencia. She climbed into bed and wished me goodnight. I was restless, because of the debate, because of the marijuana, because of the tequila, so I turned off the television and whispered into her ear as if a seraph, "My love, I think I will take a walk..."—"Hurry back." She prayed, and drifted away into her sueños de enfermos. I maudled posh grounds at 1 am, stumbling past fountains, hardscape, locked up barstools and the quiet of after hour swimming pools. An apparition in a ghost town. The only souls not abandoned in the night were a tile crew. Troweling graveyard installations. I am passionate for tile, so I haunted them for a quarter of an hour, for the lifetime of an earthly residency. Bumping and knocking, but they looked through me like gas and ceremonial smoke of some wafting offering. So, I moved my existence further into the bardo. I heard the roar of the river on the back side of an empty, commercial kitchen, so I gave up the knives at the prep table and followed its course up a climbing path, higher and higher—a propulsion—an astral projection. My safe spaces twinkled below me, far in the blurry distance, but curiosity ever kills all the cats and I reject the umbilical calling, climbing until I came upon some ancient, stacked block wall. Finding footholds, I hoisted myself over the cresting stones and peered out into the dark still waters of a wide lake, pondering the existences on the other side. What monsters live beneath this surface?? Waiting with their ravenous appetites—Ready to feed on all morsels. Drifting within their ranges—I looked back for my safety-line, but found it gone, and my heart climbs into my throat. I paddle in return on an onyx sea, surrounded by the sting of nettles and jellyfish. Splashing my way. Stilling my panic in a doubtful promise of return. Moonless black, I come upon the outline of a footbridge. Below, I can hear the rushes of hungry rapids. Furiously roaring my name out from beneath these feet. Sleep with us! Join us! Just Take A Moment! I test the tension, of the cables, and woozily sway above the voices; footstep by swinging footstep. El fuerte. Again. Again. Reaching the other end of this ordeal I come before the outline of the dark, quiet house. Looming shadow. Enormous and black as a mountain. It stands before me in the darkness as a snake-god's pyramid. Large, black windows peering into me, and the voices of the river are still toying in my cranium, demanding sacrifice. And I do not trust their invitation. "Join Us!..." I move away from these barbed promises, toward different crossroads. Like a moth, new glows draw me. Pursuing illuminations, I flutter near a lit stairwell. I contemplate the deathly silence of it. The sinecure. A raccoon, I descend into the earth. Silently spilling one cascading foot over the next foot fall—and the next, Like Orpheus—until I reached the bottom. There—a sleek modern bar. It is fully stocked and unattended. Stunning bottles of all shapes, sizes and colorful variety. All filled with booze. Promise elixirs. Of courage. Of vast, potential. I find a whisky and pull it from the rack. Crack the seal and pour the warmth of it down my throat. Absorb the sweet burn of it. I wander among empty tables of abandon. Nothing interests me here, so—I take the whisky, my adventure token, and I stumble back in search of voices.

—In the vicious, late-morning sun, my girl stands over my carcass, prodding me for proofs of life. Vitality signs. My eyes are on fire and heat is emanating through the rest of my dizzy head. The Devil's bargain with us that choose life, is suffrage.

"—We're late," she admonishes me, a naughty schoolboy, "Jean will be down in the cafe in 15 minutes."—Ah, Jean…—resident of all things in this Mexican pueblo. I had forgotten about Jean.

"Alright," I concede, wanting only to wash the rancid taste of evil from my morning mouth.

As I will myself to a sitting position, "—What is this?"—She asks.

She gestures to the shanghaied whiskey bottle on the nightstand. Prosecutorial evidence before my impending trials, and dream-threads come back to me.

"—Uh," I respond, scratching at my beard stubble, "something I found last night—while walking. I shift the subject.

At a cafe table Jean quips through my salvation of steaming Mexican Coffee. She offers perspective. History on the terra of wealth. On the Silver Trail, established, centuries ago. She tells of properties of existence, while I pour a second cup.

"What are your plans in the days to come?" She enquires. My girl tells her of the dinner reservations for that evening. A steakhouse. Jean scowls at the name of the restaurant. "It's cartel owned," she educates, "you shouldn't eat there."

"The concierge gave it very high recommendations," she defends.

Jean draws her brows together and presses her lips, "It's cartel owned."

At the restaurant, the hostess shows us to our seats, amid the many bodies and chatter that now fill the populated floor plan. Here, my apparition had walked these halls only moments ago. We are brought before the magnificence of the main entrance and seated there before the impressive libation bar with it's shining inventory—minus one whiskey bottle. I search overhead for ceiling cameras—pulling my fedora further down over my guilty eyes. I look at the prices on the menu, and I know for certain—this place is getting away with murder.

Robin Williams

Awed by the publicity of your stardom, in a crippling apprehension,
Whispering your name, the ladies proclaim you as a "good mensch."
Tired of standing, I took the only seat left open, by you on the bench.
Now sitting, we two dads, watching our kids at play, me and Robin
Williams.

O Fisher King from another planet, quiet in cellular interphase,
Even as those Lewey-body proteins conspire in the mazes
Of a genius mind. They brew brutal hallucinations, razing
The serenity of your meditative sanctuaries and safe places.

It's not that I don't wish to pepper you with the thousand questions,
Nothing original, all you've heard before; but that I respect the position
Of privacy. You are not here on display to entertain the imposition
I could level. All men deserve their space without undue confliction.

And so, the mensch and I sit, watching our offspring at play,
In the McDonald's playland structure, at Stanyan and Haight;
And while older than my sons, I must honestly admit to say,
Your children were quite kind to mine.

—And that itself, speaks volumes of the man.

Take Me To The Taj Mahal
—10/26—11/1, 2024

Legendary Rhythm & Blues,
Seven-day, Caribbean cruise,
Wash me with the music
Is it in you yet?
Like an infection.
Like an injection,
That swells and sings,
That rocks as it rolls
On the Spirit of the Sea.

Neptune give up your song,
In them 12-bar grooves
From the 1, to the 4,
To the 5-7 chords.
Tickle me like ivories.
And the animals are jumping
Thumping to the beat.
Wild as a Rainstorm,
Swinging like chimpanzees.

From the 9th floor Lido Deck
The wind flows whip a fedora
Overboard to a furious wake,
And it passes in the moment
As if, the notes from this stage;
Likewise, slipping o'er a wood rail.
Everything is a time and place.
—And we're all passing through.

At the piano bar the duel
Plays out, while Eden Brent
Is 'Sweatin' Like A Pig,
And Singin' Like A Lady.'
Rain pours on the pool deck,
Shadows darken and burgeon
During the Kingfish feeding,
smelt scurry for the sandbar.
Gimme Shelter a shot away,
Take me to the Taj Mahal.

I saw Dumpstaphunk
Move a 1-legged man
from his fettering seat,
Hobble to the dance floor,
to partake in shamanism.
The ritual beauty of tribe.
Bouncing in time, his spirit flies,
as Vanessa Collier wails in fury.
Giving Tupac and California
The Mississippi treatment.

In Chuck Barber's
Soul Lounge:
The Reverend
takes us to church.
Screaming to Sea-Gods:
"There Ain't No Party
 Like A Blues Cruise Party
 'Cos A Blues Cruise Party
 Goes Pop!!"

Joanna Collins has bent my brain,
Catharsis and inferno-chops,
She has both everything and nothing
to prove.
The wind boxes my ears, tearing at my follicle line.
And blousily I pump my fist.
Root—4—Root—6—5——
Until The Thrill Is Gone…

Bring it to me New Orleans,
Chicago, Harlem, & Texas.
Give me songs of mid-passage.
Any missed opportunities
  for conversation,
Are missed opportunities
  for unification—
These are times and tides we ride,
Durations do rise and fall together.

Recountenance

11-6-2024

In the aftermath,
In recountenance,
I now am asked,
If I have any—

Regrets. Do you?

In a suck of breath held,
Stilled before a death-drop,
MAGA Red Wave, born blood
Droplet stains on a fallen blade.

Blink, and we awaken
Shocked at this brevity,
Union torn in moral crisis,
Cancer eats at my Country.

The Bison Race

(The Tall Tale of Montana Mitch)

Beneath timber beams and taxidermy of Bullwinkle's,
One armed bandits graze behind my frontier style stool.
Montana Mitch is looking to break a bill into singles,
He notes my Gene Autry-style shirt and pint of Moose Drool.

He sniffs me out like a coyote to see where I belong.
Asks if I'm from Nashville, if I'm a singer of country songs?
"Semper Fi!" Mitch howls his trauma, indoctrinate tune,
Mad marches of his youth in Carolina's, Camp Lejune.

We are a week out before the opening of the high season,
Coastal elites, Nuts and Fruits descend as demons
On a territorial imperative his daddy did love so well.
5 ½ months of snow thaws to 5 ½ months of Tourist Hell.

The cause as to why his kids can no longer afford
Three bedrooms in Bozeman: Invasive Species;
Trails to cheaper lands in tears and relocative histories,
Spreading investment seeds like choker weeds.

Positional decorum, dance about topics and trials,
Concede to the hunter's tall tales of both the glory and grisly;
Montana Mitch's only wish is to keep the West wild.
"Exactly how close—" he eyes me, "were you to that grizzly?"

"About sixty feet," I repeat, "from that wall to that…"
Mitch notes the distance, shakes his head, "Not far enough," he spits,
"And stay away from the buffalo, grazing on the rough."
He tells both beasts will charge any naive, ambling tourist.

"Except for this one time," Mitch proceeds with a twinkle,
"My Daddy and Uncle Carlton got the best of a bison…"
"How's that?" I respond to the bait. "...When I was a child,
In the back car seat, I witnessed a wager between Daddy and Carlton,

They'd been drinkin' Huckleberry-Marys from Gardiner to meadow,
When they swerved over and cranked down the glass,
Daddy cried, 'Mitchie, just take a look out of your window!'
Certain enough, there was a magnificent bull chewing the grass.

"I'll bet you this $100," Carlton crowed, putting bill upon the dash,
"That you're too chicken shit to ride the back of that old bison!"
Daddy's head bobbled in consideration, before withdrawing at last,
His own $100 note. "Make it $200 for whichever of mother's sons

Can get there first! The manliest brother to mount the back
Takes both the pot and all the future rights of this big story brag."
Carlton grinned while he considered the match as attractive.
"Alright," he then added, "but gotta do it both, Buck-Ass-Naked!"

I watched Daddy and Carlton spit in palms and shake the deal,
Out of the passenger seat and from behind the steering wheel,
Those hairy bearded brothers stripped all the way to their boots.
Maudled into the meadow, laughing in naught but nature's suits.

"On Three!" Daddy's impaired toe dug and traced a starting line:
"One, Two, *Three*!"—Laughing all ass and elbows they did run,
Straight at that bull who stopped at feed to see a loss of two minds,
Arms and penises flailing, whooping and hollering, "*Hi-Yaw, Bison!*!"

—Now, I can't be certain what was in the mind of that noble beast,
—Seeing two scrawny mountain men coming in upon a suicidal track,
Perhaps he thought them ill or a predatorial variety: Cute & Petite?
But one thing is for certain: The bull knew he wanted none-to-do with *that!*

He turned and gave tail, speeding off across the frozen plane,
Leaving Daddy and Carlton beyond all hope. The chase abandoned,
They let loose the laughs of lunatics, both intoxicated and insane,
And that's how they ever clung to claim, that night: *They'd Bested That Old Bison!*

The Floating Head Of Jesus Christ

Jesus….
Your disembodied head
Floats in the space
Commended into my hands.
Bright, shiny gift wrap,
Cloaked promise and festoon
Of ribbons and bows.
I tear into paper like a flagellation.
Seeking some landslide salvation,
Bringing your skull here to my hands.
I did not decree John's tongue
Before me on this platter.
Death reeks … Holy Ghost.
Lead sketched eyes that seek
Divination and enlightenment.
Rolling toward your traitorous father
And the crimson streams
That drop from thy halo of thorns,
Pressed like talons upon your crown.
And your rolling eyes follow me…
A voyeuristic kink: Watching me—
Seeing me—Knowing cellophane secrets.
Fucking Pervert!
I hang you like a crucifixion.
Suspended on the bedroom wall
Solitude and sanctuary—my cell.
Behind the framed glass,
Beneath the judgment of
Your knowing agonized face.
I give you a commiserative wink,
And spark another blunt;
As we both die of thirst.

Tocar

Like a spider, fingers crawl & traverse across the fretboard.
Spindly, spindly, digit meat mixed with nail tonality.
Bleed for me note, Bleed!
Trill and hammer and pull, quiver for me with your vibrato.
49 Notes of Ecstasy.
While I run my hands along your curvatures.
Scream for me.
Open your throat.
Resonate,
High and sustained,
 A tocar.
 Scream.

Chronicles of Central Mexico

1. San Miguel de Allende

In the termalicas of La Gruta,
I find myself 6,000 feet above sea level. Equidistant
between the cyclical flows of the Pacific and el Caribe.
As waters splash in cascading pools,
And the skies are now awash in vapor white,
The breezes caress my skin and encourage my stillness.
—Think on nothing.
—Today Time Shall Wait…
—Hijo de la Terra.

In the high desert of San Miguel de Allende
Spanish voices and great-tailed grackles coo in retreat.
Hidalgo's voice rides the wind from the square at Atotonilco,
Before the nave and master painted ceilings of a Sistine inspire.
At the Zocola the mariachis blare their brass
in a competition of economics.
The pious exit beneath the spires of the Parroquia—
and sombreros are passed por las propensias.

I am sitting in the back of the taxi—
A converted Honda Fit,
The hard shell maletas are rattling
in the trunk.
Rattling like cannon shots in my ears. Deafening. The driver is talking at me.
A relentless, unstoppable flow,
His eyes dart up at me in the rear-view mirror…
I feel compelled to respond, "Si!"—And the flow continues.
Covering the details of what? I have no idea??

I am in a crush of humanity, beneath the terra cotta tiled roofs,
Testing the suspension of an aged bus. Barreling downhill in return
from the Mercado Martes toward the Jardin at the Centro.
Stoically—cobble stones rattle all of our bones.

An opaque light covers a mangle of brown limbs clutching at grab bars,
bolted tightly to the arched mobile ceiling, as a Mexican flag waves above
the rear bumper in both pride and defiance. When the driver does deign to
brake, beneath the *giant crucifixion* over his sun visor, the wind ceases to fly

the nylon colors of red, white and green, and for a moment the waning sun fills this chaliced vessel of population.

Las gentes comonales.

2. Sur de Queretero

Swaths of clouds
Dominate this arched
Ceiling. A blitz.
Arco de la catedral.
Naturales.

Though defenseless
beneath sheer volume
Neither blue agave,
Nor nestles of maize
seem to shrink from
either the threat or promise
of an impending aguacero,
The flashes and downpours
That come furiously hard,
They charge and exhilarate
these animals…
Las vacas y caballos,
in the lush rough carve
of the valley of Queretaro.

Crack you beasts! Crack!
Release your rushes—
—Deal us your worst.

3. Mexico City Blues

242 Choruses of shit.
Mexico City Blues.
As I bus into Mexico Valley
from San Miguel, I find myself

thinking, "Man, I'll Never
Get Those Hours Back!"

If Kerouac is a jazz poet—
Laying down hard riffs
of improvisational language
and timbre and tone…
He doesn't know the phrase
or key of his own song—

—And I can feel the stone glares
In the shadows of Zinco Jazz Club
of Prado, Tenorio Jr. and Esquivel.

4. El Sacramento

Power lines begin to gather
in force above brick and block abodes.
And the skies of Mexico Valley are once again, cracking…
White flashes rend and retreat,
pledging harder moments to come.
From the top deck of a plush bus, behind the glass
I can see the gravel loads and semi exhaust at eye level.
Overpasses cover me like a net and Los Angeles springs to mind.
A las cinco en la tarde….
And wheels grind to laborious halts.
And it takes my taxi an hour and 45 minutes to cross this town.

Mira! The box stores conspire like a breeding ground.
Billboards and concrete. Viva Mexico!
Construction cranes and overlaps of domiciles cover
the hillsides of the Valley.
Henry George warned, "Man is nothing without the land."
Here la gente scramble for footholds in the heart of chaos.
OXXO and Michelin Tires, Fissured asphalts and Frida Khalo.

Hordes of homeless are encamped along Calle Paganini.
And I can hear the banda. The tuba, the accordion.
I dreamt last night of an eagle who dropped a snake at my feet.

The bird seemed to be in my head like a telepathy.
Seeking me above arrid desert sands for 28 days,
Before sighting me in the Valley and diving for my legs.
When I stood mute with no response, the bird retrieved the serpent,
And enigmatically disappeared into a void like a lost civilization.
I sought interpretation to this vision in the sinking stones
Of the Basilica de Guadalupe, praying to the East,
Getting no closer to understanding the faiths lost in my childhood.

Once, and again, and again, a continuum…
The lightning flashes ricochet off the sides of the high rises
outside the plate glass window of my hotel room.
Thunder demands like an Aztec drumming,
These Gods require blood sacrifice.

And it occurs to me….
You can never understand Mexico until you've suckled the breast of this City.
        Which you will never capture.
        Never dominate.
Otra vez, the skies split in a white flash.
It blinds you, like the rush of a spike
And the deluge comes.
It pours over you, drenching your clothes,
The penetrating squish of socks within your boots,
Water spills from the brim of your hat,
and your baptism begins.

Waking The Neighbors

I want to be a denizen
Of your heated backyard living,

Where the mad buzz
Of hummingbird wings strafe at scalps.

Where you eat, and sleep,
While wetted petals are pressed apart.

I want to devour that bud.
Venus nestled between your thighs,

Stripping your mind bare,
Establish a residency in your third eye.

Seducing me in similes…

And I want so very much,
To be the tongue of that church bell,

Landing in swing against
The edges of your warmed, concave swell

Waking the neighbors,
Wondering if they've missed Sunday service?

Fucked Up

In the end we had found an Arco,
Somewhere just off Sepulveda,
They stocked cheap plastic sunglasses
To cut the glare that was splitting my head.
Jagged barbs bored into my brain matter,
After a missed connection at LAX.
Behind these gentler shaded visuals,
And with the hip flask in my pocket,
The world was a more tolerable place.

The improvement must have been readable,
Gassing off the scent of approachability.
The hard luck case drifted within our range,
Sniffed us out in a parking lot which had seen brighter days.
He hit us with an olid stench of body odor and grift.
"Hey Boss," he said, "You got a dollar,
So's I can buy me some gas?
I gotta gets me up to The Valley."

"No," I dismissed him—but he wasn't
Going to be put off as easily as that.
Certainly he knew the game better than I.
And maybe he did? Or maybe he didn't?
He sought the better footing,
"Look at this shit my mother did to me!"
He suddenly lifted his stained T-shirt,
Exposing the jigsaw of violent scars
That criss-crossed his lean torso.

"Huh?"—Though impressive, I remained
Immovable, "That's fucked up."
I took a slug of whisky and passed
The flask to my lady-friend.
She expressed more tolerance than I,
"Your mother did that to you!?"
"Shit!" He confirmed, "You Goddamn Right,
She Did!! Cut Me With A Knife!'
He chopped at the air for emphasis.
"That's fucked up." She equated,
And came over to my side of the fence.
Neitchsze warned of the dangers of empathy.

She swallowed a slug and handed me
Back the ration of liquor.
He must have thought we two crackers
Were as thick as a loaf of sourdough.
A dollar or five, would have been enough
To have bought back our peace of mind.
Banish him away in satisfaction,
Toll fees, taxes, and alms for the poor.
He would need to personalize the pitch.

"That's A Nice Shirt!" he flattered
My fashion choices. A basic Hawaiian
Button down of palm and paradise print.
"You Buy That In Hawaii!?" He was
Looking to assess my financial net-worth.
A man who can afford the golden sands,
High-rise hotels and the luaus of Waikiki.
"No." I clinched the topic.
"No?" He challenged, "Then Where?
Where Did You Get It!??"

"I found it, in my closet," I leveled.
"Really??"—That caught my girl's interest.
"Yeah," I repeated, wondering where
We might find the next watering hole,
"It wasn't mine, and it certainly didn't belong
To the kids. —My guess is that it belonged
To my wife's boyfriend, likely she got confused
And hung it up with my wardrobe.
—Lucky for me—we're the same size."
"And so now you're wearing it?"
She smirked.
"Well—It's a nice shirt," I justified.
A beat of silence before the grifter spoke,
"Man—That's Fucked Up!"

Boots

In the arrid breeze I swung my crocs,
Across that crumbled, concrete walk.
Terra smell of sand and rattlesnake,
Run rabbit run—Fly and stay awake,
Shake your scent from flicking tongue,
Death sleeps in the desert—rabbit run!

El hombre was still beneath a blinding sun,
Sombrero tipped to shade those slumbering
Eyes, above bleach, rat-torn tennis shoes,
Crossed at the ankles. My shadow soon
Choked beams that piped an empty tip jar,
And further warped the roughed up guitar,

Across his lap. I drew $20 from my pocket,
Dropped it in the glass and then looked at
The portrait before me. Soil-caked. Hombre.
He opened one eye, "Play a song for me,"
I challenged, rousing him to a straighter sit.
He adjusted the tuning, leaned over and spit.

"What do you want to hear?" He croaked.
"A song of your heart—a song of the road..."
Theatrics are tiresome. So, he let out a sigh,
Before exotic footwear caught coveting eye,
"Nice Boots!" Reaction he could not contain.
"You like those?" I folded into conversation.

"Yeah..." He raised the pitch of the G String,
Projecting away to another place of meaning.
I awaited his return from that far away place,
"I had me some nice boots once..." His face
Held a story, "But that was a long time ago.."
"You know," I followed, "Boots come and go."

"Yeah," he smiled, "...Boots come and go."

Surquedry

(2024, Poem of alarm)

Whatchu know 'bout this!?
Cried an incensed Van Zant.
Perhaps Southern Man ought
Learn to keep his head…

Screaming and crosses burning
In a Young and brave new world.
But I love you, Brother. *Bring it!*
Your culture. Your 1st line parade.

I am not my dead people's baggage.
  —Are you?
    —Ethos of those Southern gentlemen
      Who came before.
In these United States.

On a stool in the Quarter,
steps from Jackson Square,
He tells me, "That's my opinion,
…As a Southern Gentleman."

Backed by his army, his colors,
his election denying President,
he takes up the mantle of champion
in these culture wars.

—And I can smell the bourbon on his breath.

"Tell me again, where y'all from?"
"San Francisco," I amiably repeat.
"Frisco is a shit-hole," he goads again.
"Dude, San Francisco Is *Amazing*!" I correct.

"Naw," he tells me, "this here is amazing."
"Yes," I agree, "New Orleans is amazing.
It's as Tennesse Williams once stated,
There are 3 cities in the United States…"
"San Francisco is a Shit-Hole!!"
He rises from his stool and leans in

With his weight, his youth and ire,
"And That is my Opinion, as a Southern Gentleman."

"Sure," I dead-eye the asshole back,
so as to be sure, not to be misunderstood,
"But you must understand…
—Nobody Cares about your Opinion."

—Damned Cog.

And I can feel the gassing off, of all
this indignation, all this hostility.
His ineffective intimidation tactics.
No idea of the battles behind me.

Will this surquedric bear swing?
Crush me as his effigy, leftist totem?
I am his representative of Pelosi,
Gun Control, and Big Government,

By mere means of geography:
—You are what you eat.
—You are where you come from…
—So—I let the Fresno come out.

I reach for my fine silver fork,
next to the black linen napkin.
Casually, I grip it like an ice pick
and I prepare myself to swing
these tines into his throat,
as sour, conservative anger
radiates against my back.

Mark Novak is a writer who works primarily from the San Francisco/ Bay Area. He holds an M.A. in Creative Writing and Poetry from San Francisco State University. His work has been featured in the *Monterey Poetry Review, The Miserere Review, The Lothlorien Journal of Poetry, The Bards West and San Francisco Anthologies* and the *Cocktales Literary Pages of DearBooze.com*. His work, 'The Vagabond Quothe Shakespeare' was the 6th place finalist in the *Writer's Digest* National Poetry Awards (2017). He is both a voice talent for readings and a contributing writer for the poetry database, *Voetica.com*. *Sonnets For Agnodice* with Finishing Line Press is his debut chapbook.

www.ingramcontent.com/pod-product-compliance
Lightning Source LLC
LaVergne TN
LVHW090540110826
845146LV00003B/1191

* 9 7 9 8 8 9 9 9 0 4 8 3 7 *